# RECHARGE:

*Devotional bible study methods to recharge your spiritual growth, improve your spiritual health, & grow your intimacy with God.*

# by Carey Green

*www.ChristianHomeandFamily.com*

*Printed in the United States of America - Published by Christian Home and Family - Copyright © 2014 Carey Green - All rights reserved.*

*No part of this book may be reproduced in any form or by any electronic or mechanical means including information storage and retrieval systems, without permission in writing from the author. The only exception is by a reviewer, who may quote short excerpts in a review.*

*Unless otherwise noted, scripture quotations are from The Holy Bible, English Standard Version® (ESV®), copyright © 2001 by Crossway, a publishing ministry of Good News Publishers. Used by permission. All rights reserved.*

*Visit www.ChristianHomeandFamily.com for more resources like this.*

# *Other books by this author*

### NON-FICTION

**The Marriage Improvement Project**
a devotional study for couples
http://amzn.com/B00A6Z5K9A

**The Elder Training Handbook**
an assessment and training tool for the local church
http://amzn.com/1475137559

### FICTION

**The Great Smizzmozzel Bash**
a rhyming, rollicking adventure for kids (picture book)

**Moving Toward God:** Finding God from Square One: A Newbie's Guide to the Basics of Christianity
http://amzn.com/B00LCKNRHU

**Dragon Slayer: Beginnings**
a Christian fantasy novel (releasing March, 2014)
http://www.dragonslayerbook.com

Keep up to date with Carey's writing pursuits at his website:
www.ChristianHomeandFamily.com/store1

# TABLE OF CONTENTS

People who deserve some credit

Why I wrote this book

What you will find in this book

### SECTION ONE: MINDSET

<u>Mindset #1: Set Your Mind</u>

> *Here's where I cover the foundational step to a successful devotional/quiet time with God. It's all mental. You've got to be thinking right about what you're doing so that it doesn't turn into legalism on one hand or a pointless activity on the other.*

<u>Mindset #2: Make a Plan</u>

> *This is where most people miss the quiet time boat. They dive into the deep end without any kind of idea of how they're going to swim. Don't do that. Learn how to come up with a plan that works for you.*

<u>Mindset #3: Don't Let the Plan Become a Straight-Jacket</u>

> *Having a plan is good (I just wrote a whole chapter on the subject). But don't let the plan become something that limits your time with God. This mindset can help you avoid a ton of frustration.*

<u>Mindset #4: Simple Mind Hacks</u>

> *There are a lot of simple, common-sense, basic approaches to your daily time with God that you need*

*to get into your head. This section covers some of them.*

## Common Mindset Mistakes

*This section fills you in on the common mindset mistakes people make regarding their daily devotions. I wonder how many of these you'll recognize in yourself...*

## SECTION TWO: METHODS

### Method #1: The S.O.A.P. Method

*This method is simple, easy to do, and something you can accomplish daily. I guarantee it. I have to give credit to Pastor Wayne Cordiero for this one.*

### Method #2: The Scripture Prayer Method

*I absolutely LOVE this method. It combines scripture reading with prayer to provide a powerful tool in your "get to know God better" tool box.*

### Method #3: The Topical Study Method

*If you want to know a biblical topic really, really well, this is the method for you. WARNING: The topical method can take a very long time, but it's worth it.*

### Method #4: The Journaling Method

*If you are a writer or like to work out your thoughts on paper, this is the method for you. I can't fully explain how beneficial journaling has been to my spiritual life.*

### Method #5: The Questions Method

*Learning to ask good questions about what you're reading can open up the depths of understanding. You'll want to read this chapter.*

## Method #6: The 30 Day Per Book Method

*My oldest daughter taught me about this study method, and it's a great way to get into the heart of a particular Bible book over a 30 day period. I dare you to try it.*

## Method #7: A Prayer System that Works

*One of the biggest frustrations for me when it comes to prayer has been how to keep up with my ever-growing list of prayer requests in a way that seems manageable. Here's how I've attempted to meet the challenge.*

## **SECTION THREE: WRAP UP**

## My "normal" Daily Quiet Time System

*I'm hesitant to show you exactly what I do each day because I don't want you to think there's any kind of "magic" in it... but you're smarter than that. You'll understand this is just ONE of many ways to approach quiet time, so I hope it helps.*

## You can do this

*My final words of encouragement.*

# PEOPLE WHO DESERVE SOME CREDIT

**Wayne Cordiero** - pastor of New Hope Church in Hawaii is the one from whom I learned the "S.O.A.P." study method contained in chapter (##). You can find the way their church applies the S.O.A.P. Bible study method at http://www.enewhope.org/nextsteps/journaling/.

**My mother** - she's... well, my mom. Her consistent example and loving encouragement to search the scriptures for myself has played an enormous part in shaping my spiritual life. Thanks Mom!

**My wife** - Next to my salvation, Mindi is my greatest blessing on this earth. God has used her to teach me so much about life, love, relationships, and the application of the scriptures. I KNOW that her fingerprints are all over the content of this book. Thanks Babe. I love you more.

# WHY I WROTE THIS BOOK

Every author has a reason for the books he/she writes... even if it's an undefined urge that compels them to grab a paper and pen. I know. I've been writing things off and on, in journals, on computers, and in notebooks for years, and I always had a reason.

I want you to know, very clearly, why I wrote this book.

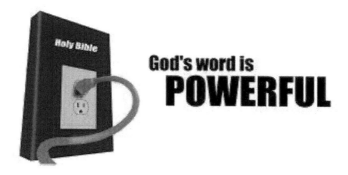

I wrote this book because I have come to see that God's word is powerful, so powerful that when it's rightly understood and applied, it can transform your life!

> **Hebrews 4:12 - For the word of God is living and active, sharper than any two-edged sword, piercing to the division of soul and of spirit, of joints and of marrow, and discerning the thoughts and intentions of the heart.**

Notice the words used there. They are NOT words used of any other book.

- *living*

- *active*
- *dividing soul and spirit*
- *discerning the thoughts and intentions of the heart*

There is no doubt about it… the Bible has a very unique power to it.

<u>*But don't misunderstand…*</u>

The Bible is not ebbing with power just sitting on your shelf or bedside table. It's got to be used.

And… contrary to what many people think… even when it's used, it won't always transform the one who reads it. The Bible's power comes to life when you apply what it says to your life.

That means you have to let it shape the way you think, the way you feel, and the way you behave. You have to commit yourself to putting into practice what it teaches you to do.

Jesus said so Himself…

> **<u>Luke 6:47-49</u> – Everyone who comes to me and hears my words and does them, I will show you what he is like: he is like a man building a house, who dug deep and laid the foundation on the rock. And when a flood arose, the stream broke against that house and could not shake it, because it had been well built. But the one who hears and does not do them is like a man who built a house on the ground without a foundation. When the stream broke against it, immediately it fell, and the ruin of that house was great**

In over twenty years of ministry as a local church Pastor, I ran into person after person after person who either *didn't know how to go about studying their Bible, or didn't know how to apply it.*

This book is written to help you do both, in easy to understand, practical ways… because that is the ***only way*** you are going to be transformed.

**I'M HERE TO HELP**

One last thing.

I'm not an author who stays cloistered away in a mysterious writing retreat someplace. I am a real person, just like you. I struggle, grow, and experience the hardships and joys of life. Just like you.

**I am happy to help...**

All that to say, I'm here to help. If you'd like to interact about the things in this book… feel free to contact me. I DO respond to my email. (carey@careygreen.com)

# WHAT YOU WILL FIND IN THIS SHORT BOOK

What lies ahead are two sections, each focused on a different aspect of what it takes to get the most out of your time with God as you study His word. The two sections are:

- *Mindsets*
- *Methods*

Let's talk about each of those for a moment…

**MINDSETS** are the things that "run" you… your software, so to speak. Your mindsets have to do with what you believe more than anything.

When you approach God's word and time with Him, there are some very key mindsets you need to have in place in order for your time with Him to truly be beneficial. If you don't then you will be more prone to running into the "dryness" that we've all experienced in our quiet times with the LORD.

So… don't skip the mindset section. It's foundational to the other stuff that follows.

**METHODS** are the ways you go about doing things, the patterns you follow to enable you to accomplish whatever it is that you're trying to accomplish.

When it comes to spending good, quality time with the LORD, you *will* default to some method whether you know it or not. Even if you are trying to have a "Spirit-led" time with Him that has very little structure, you *will* have a structure nonetheless. We are creatures of habit and will put some kind of format in place to govern the routine of our lives. That includes our daily time that we set apart for communing with God.

So, it seems wise to me that if I'm going to have a pattern in place by default, it would be best for me to *be intentional* about what that pattern is. How do I do that without logic-ing the thing to death in my own human strength?

I ask the LORD to guide me and believe Him to do that… even in something as simple and mundane as choosing a practical tool to help arrange my time with Him (like the tools you'll find in the methods section of this book).

When you get there, you'll find the methods section is full of easy-to-learn, practical methods of Bible study and prayer. I outline these briefly, give you some of the pros and cons of the method, and in most cases, provide an example of how it might look when it's carried out.

Keep in mind, (back to the mindset) that these are tools, not laws or requirements or handcuffs. They are designed to be of help, not be a hindrance. If you find any of the tools listed in the methods section are not helpful to your goal of drawing near to God, then stop using it, at least for a while. Freshness is often a key to keeping our time with the LORD vibrant, and switching methods from time to time can do give a "refresh" at times.

## ONE LAST THING BEFORE YOU BEGIN

Being a disciple of Jesus Christ is about relationship much more than it is about routine, rules, methods, or mindsets. You have to understand that. It's so important I'm going to say it again.

Being a disciple of Jesus Christ is about relationship.

When you engage in a daily quiet time or devotional time, you are coming to a PERSON; Jesus Christ, LORD of the universe. You are seeking to know Him, to hear from Him, to be guided by Him. He is the greatest personality to ever enter human history, with no exception… and you have the honor of spending time with Him every day.

Let that truth (and it is true) guide you every day as you engage in the practice of daily devotions.

Now, it's time to get recharged.

I will only count this effort at writing a success if you put this book down and pick up your Bible… with a greater sense of how to understand it and how to apply it to your own life.

If you do that, I'm confident you'll begin to experience transformation in your own life. You'll sense a ***RECHARGE*** in your relationship with Christ.

**Carey Green**
January, 2014

*SECTION ONE: MINDSET*

# *MINDSET #1: SET YOUR MIND*

I'm learning more and more that the way I think dramatically impacts the way that I live.

Think about it... (get it?) That very phrase tells us that life is largely governed by the way we think about and approach the things we encounter day to day.

Before we get too far into this, let me clarify what I mean.

**I'm NOT talking about** the naïve and stupid notion that you can "create your own reality" by governing what you think on and what you don't. There are Christian-ized versions of that kind of nonsense. It teaches that that faith itself is a force that can be governed by what you believe, and ultimately what you speak. (Kenneth Copeland, "The Force of Faith": Kenneth Copeland Publications, 1983".

Like I said, it is nonsense and I warn you to stay away from that kind of teaching. Far away.

Reality as we know it is governed by God alone. He is the sovereign over the universe, not you or me. So get it OUT of your head that you can change or create reality by having "positive thoughts" or "positive energy." It's not true. It doesn't happen that way.

**What I AM talking about** is this: *What you believe matters.*

*If you believe what is truly true*, your life is being guided down a path that follows the course of reality. You are going to learn, grow, and develop the ability to understand God, life, and the way the two relate to each other. You'll live in a more secure place ultimately.

*If you believe what is false* (untrue, a lie), your life is being guided down a path that follows away from the course of reality. You're going to get confused, lost, and ultimately be far, far away from God, who is truth.

All of that is just another way to say what Jesus said in **John 8:32**

**…you will know the truth, and the truth will set you free.**

When you know what is really true, you are free to begin living without the entanglements of:

- *Misconceptions*
- *Lies*
- *False beliefs*

To paraphrase Jesus (and yes, I'm very cautious about doing that)…

*If the truth can set you free, then lies can put you in bondage.*

That is exactly why…

## MINDSET IS HUGE

This should not be surprising to us. The Apostle Paul told us how important mindset is:

> **<u>Romans 12:2</u> - Do not be conformed to this world, but be transformed by the renewal of your mind, that by testing you may discern what is the will of God, what is good and acceptable and perfect.**

In this verse Paul mentions two amazing things that a right, transformed mindset can produce.

- *<u>Personal transformation</u>*

This point is truly amazing, so take a little time to ponder it. The essence of who you and I are as human beings can be changed if we think rightly. ***Changed.***

If you've ever given up on a New Year's resolution, failed on a diet or exercise plan, or bailed out on trying to break a bad habit, then you know, *accomplishing personal transformation is no small thing*.

In this passage God is telling… no, He's ***promising***, that as we present our bodies to Him as living sacrifices (*vs. 1*), and work with His help to renew our minds, *we* can be like Jesus. The mind is critical to that process.

- *<u>Knowledge of God's will</u>*

How many times have you wondered what God's will is for you, your life, or a particular situation? If you're like me, the answer is in the hundreds!

Through the pen of the Apostle Paul, God is telling us that we can ***know*** His will when our minds are renewed to ***think*** according to His ways. That's how we are able to test and discern what is good, what is acceptable to God, and what is truly perfect in each circumstance. That is an amazing promise!

## AGAIN, MINDSET IS HUGE

Without the right way of thinking, you and I will fritter our lives away. We'll default to immature, emotionally-driven, selfish thinking that does no good for anyone and falls miserably short of what God intends for us to accomplish in life.

Just to drive the point a bit more deeply into your mind, here's a quick list of passages from the New Testament that tell us how important the mind is, with a few brief observations of my own.

<u>Pleasing God depends on our mindset</u>

**Romans 8:5-8** – **For those who live according to the flesh set their minds on the things of the flesh, but those who live according to the Spirit set their minds on the things of the Spirit. For to set the mind on the flesh is death, but to set the mind on the Spirit is life and peace. For the mind that is set on the flesh is hostile to God, for it does not submit to God's law; indeed, it cannot. Those who are in the flesh cannot please God.**

Did you hear that? You and I *cannot* please God if our mind is on the wrong things.

<u>*We cannot become "new" without the right mindset*</u>

**Ephesians 4:17-24** – **Now this I say and testify in the Lord, that you must no longer walk as the Gentiles do, in the futility of their minds. They are darkened in their understanding, alienated from the life of God because of**

**the ignorance that is in them, due to their hardness of heart. They have become callous and have given themselves up to sensuality, greedy to practice every kind of impurity. But that is not the way you learned Christ – assuming that you have heard about him and were taught in him, as the truth is in Jesus, to put off your old self, which belongs to your former manner of life and is corrupt through deceitful desires, and to be renewed in the spirit of your minds, and to put on the new self, created after the likeness of God in true righteousness and holiness.**

There are quite a few things to notice from this passage about the importance of our minds.

- *A mind that is not right is a futile mind.*
- *It produces a darkened understanding.*
- *It alienates a person from the life of God.*
- *It makes them a calloused person who gives themselves up to evil.*
- *But a person who learns to follow Christ has the hope that they can become renewed in the spirit of their mind – and wonderful things result!*

<u>A "Jesus-kind-of-life" begins with the right mindset</u>

**Philippians 2:5 – Have this mind among yourselves, which is yours in Christ Jesus.**

After this verse, Paul goes on to describe a lifestyle of service to other believers that each of us should be aiming toward. It's the same type of life that Jesus lived when He was on the earth. That kind of life begins for us where it began for Jesus, with our mindset.

*Our mindset is our individual responsibility*

**Colossians 3:2-3** – **Set your minds on things that are above, not on things that are on earth. For you have died, and your life is hidden with Christ in God.**

We have a responsibility to do something specific with our minds. We can't just "float" (my wife said I was a "floater" when we first got married) and we can't just veg (pronounced "vej"). We are to set our minds where they are supposed to be. That means we have to keep them off of earthly things and place them on heavenly things.

Why is it so important that our minds are to be completely off of earthly things? Paul says it's because the earth is no longer our home. In fact, our very life exists in heaven, hidden with Christ, in God. Jesus wants us to learn how to think about ourselves according to the truth of who He has made us to be. We are now citizens of heaven, not earth. That is why we are to have our minds set on heavenly things.

*Our mindset effects whether or not we accept God's truth*

**2 Timothy 3:8** – **Just as Jannes and Jambres opposed Moses, so these men also oppose the truth, men corrupted in mind and disqualified regarding the faith.**

Paul uses this Old Testament account to remind Timothy that a corrupted mind causes people to oppose the truth, God's truth.

*The right mindset makes us ready for Jesus to fulfill His promises*

**<u>1 Peter 1:13</u> – Therefore, preparing your minds for action, and being sober-minded, set your hope fully on the grace that will be brought to you at the revelation of Jesus Christ.**

When Jesus returns we will experience the fullness of every promise He has made. That hope is something we have to keep in mind as we live out the rest of our earthly existence. Doing so prepares our minds for action in this life. If we don't do so, we won't be ready for what comes our way.

The point of this list is that our mindset matters!

## PREPARE YOUR MIND FOR ACTION

I want to borrow Peter's phrase and encourage you to prepare your mind for action as you work through the rest of this book. You need to have the right mindset about what you are trying to do when you approach meeting with God daily.

The Bible is filled from cover to cover with God's truth. It is powerful to transform (*Hebrews 4:12*). So, as you read the rest of this book learn to think of the serious thing that you are attempting to do.

You are attempting to:

- *Meet daily with the God of the universe.*
- *Read from His word, which is truth in its fullest sense.*
- *Receive guidance and clarity from Him.*
- *Respond to Him in faith and obedience so that your life is not built on sand.*

## ONE LAST MINDSET ADJUSTMENT

In the second section of this book, you are going to learn a handful of methods you can use to approach your study of the Bible. **But there is no magic in the methods.** As we've seen, the real "magic" is in your mindset.

So take a few moments. Take the next hour, and think through what you really believe about the Bible. Here's a little assignment to help you do that.

\*\*\*\*\*

**ASSIGNMENT #1**- Answer the following questions honestly...

- *Do you truly believe that the Bible is the means through which God has revealed Himself to mankind?*
- *Do you believe the Bible contains truth, as GOD sees it?*
- *Do you believe that as you rightly understand and apply it, the Bible can change you and your life?*
- *Do you believe that God speaks to people (like you) through His scriptures?*

If your answer to any or all of those questions is "yes," then answer this final question...

- *Is there anything on this earth (weariness, exhaustion, sickness, busy schedules, etc.) that should be allowed to keep you from spending time getting to know God and His ways through the study of the Bible?*

## ONE LAST THING

<u>Remember:</u> The following chapters will be of no lasting help to you if you don't begin with the right mindset. You need to know that you know that you know that God will meet you as you open His Bible.

It won't always be...

- *something you feel...*
- *something obvious...*
- *something life-altering (at that moment)*

... but it will be working, step by step, moment by moment to transform you and direct your life.

Set your mind.

# MINDSET #2: MAKE A PLAN

This chapter begins at square #1. It's what far too many of us Christians miss when we think about developing, strengthening, or encouraging spiritual health (*in us or our children*).

We fail to make a plan.

Think about how crucial a plan really is...

Nothing that you really want to do or need to do happens by accident. You have to do it purposely, intentionally.

Drawing close to the LORD through a quiet time with Him (*known as daily devotions, to some*) is no exception. With God's help, **you** will have to make it happen.

And you can't do that without a plan.

To some people planning may sound unspiritual, but it's not.

In fact, Paul said that one of the wonderful things the Holy Spirit produces in the life of the believer is "self control." Let's look at it for a minute...

**Galatians 5:22-23** – But the fruit of the Spirit is love, joy, peace, patience, kindness, goodness, faithfulness, gentleness, self-control; against such things there is no law.

Why do **you** think Paul includes self-control in this list (besides the obvious reason that God intends for it to be there)? I believe it's because every single one of us need self-control in order to do what we need to do to be growing closer to Jesus.

The discipline we need in order to consistently meet in a quiet time with the LORD requires the Spirit's fruit of self-control. It's self-control that enables us to be purposeful. It's self-control that empowers us to make a plan.

*And if all this talk about self-control sounds discouraging to you, take heart, it's not as dismal as you might think.*

The marvelous news for all of us sinful humans is that self-control is a fruit of the Spirit of God. That means that HE produces it in you, and for you. Your only responsibility is to walk in it as He provides it (that's called faith). It's not easy... but it is pretty simple. Think of it this way...

If I were to tell you that I have placed 3 trillion dollars in a bank account for you, and I gave you the address of the bank where it is on deposit, and I wrote down the account number for you... what would you have to do in order to take advantage of that gift?

You'd have to do two very basic things...

- *You'd have to believe me, and...*
- *You'd have to DO something to show that you believe me. In this case, you'd have to go to the bank and GET the money!*

Notice the spiritual parallel...

- *We need to believe God when He tells us that He provides self-control to us*
- *We have to do something to put our belief into action... we have to "go get" the self-control, by ACTING like it's true.*

Don't misunderstand what I mean when I say you need to "act" like it's true. I'm not talking about pretending. I'm talking about acting upon what you know to be true.

God has said it. He has promised it. We can believe it. And if we believe it, we have every reason in the world to act on that truth. That means we need to ACT out the self-control He's given us. That's called obedience.

\*\*\*\*\*

## ASSIGNMENT #2:

- *Re-read Galatians 5:22-23,*
- *Spend some time thinking about the fact that God has truly given you the gift of self-control.*
- *Picture in your mind what it would look like if you acted out your God-given self-control.*
- *Wrap up in prayer, asking God to make you able to act out what you just imagined.*

## OK, TIME TO MAKE THAT PLAN

Don't expect that you'll somehow "fit in" your personal time with the LORD from day to day.

You won't. Believe me, you won't. Here's what will happen:

- *The urgent demands of life will overwhelm your schedule and press out the truly important things, like dedicated time with the LORD.*
- *And... you have an enemy (Satan) who will do everything he can to distract, detract from, and demolish your day so that you will not have time to spend with the LORD.*

Don't give yourself any excuses… you need to plan the time you're going to spend with the LORD if you are going to grow closer to Him.

And might I suggest you make it a daily appointment?

In my experience, if I don't shoot for time with the LORD every day, my week will wind up with more days where I did not meet with Him than days where I did.

**Consistency is your ally**. That's how you build good habits in action and thinking.

Your body will even get into the act as you set a regular time for quiet with the LORD. You will become used to that time of study, and you will make good use of it as a result.

An example from my own life: I have found that the only time I can truly have quiet, alone time with God is early in the morning. I'm not saying that's when you need to schedule yours, that's just what has worked for me. Over time, as I've been consistent, my body actually wakes itself up a few minutes before my alarm goes off. I try to spend that early awake time lying in bed, preparing myself for my time with God. But that's a bit premature... we'll cover that in chapter 3. The point I'm making is that even my body is getting into the act as I stick to my plan.

So... don't let your week slip away... make a plan to spend time with the LORD daily.

I also strongly encourage you to organize your quiet time with the LORD.

Too often Christians pick up their Bibles without any idea of what they are going to read or study. They resort to an favorite passage, or flop open their Bible and begin to read wherever the pages separate.

I have two questions about approaching it that way:

- *Doesn't the Lord deserve a more diligent effort than that?*
- *Don't you need something from God each day that fits the current circumstances of your life?*

Get started

It's up to you to make the time to be along with God, and to organize a plan.

And it's up to you to stick with it. A wonderful plan that you don't follow won't do you any good.

\*\*\*\*\*

## ASSIGNMENT #3:

- *Look over your average day. When is the time of day that you are most likely to get some quiet, uninterrupted time with God?*
- *Consider the cost you'll have to pay to make that time happen. You might have to rearrange some things or get up earlier.*

- *Decide what time you're going to meet with God each day, and make a commitment to yourself.*
- *Pray, and ask Him to help you meet your commitment.*

We'll get to what goes into your plan in section two of this book.

# MINDSET #3: DON'T LET THE PLAN BECOME A STRAIGHT-JACKET

You know what a straight-jacket is, don't you? It's that stylish coat that mental institutions and law enforcement officials used to use (and sometimes still do) to make sure that an individual under their care is immobilized. A person in a straight-jacket has no use of their arms, because they are strapped into the position of a permanent self-hug.

**As good as your plan is, it can become a hindrance to you...**

Though a plan is a good thing (I said that in the previous chapter, right?), they can and often do become a straight-jackets for those who use them.

As I've thought about it, I've come to believe this happens because of some very simple mindset mistakes... yes, we're still talking about mindset.

### STRAIGHT-JACKET #1 – BELIEVING THAT THE PLAN IS "IT"

I mentioned this in the last chapter, but I want to drive the point home a bit more. The plan itself is nothing more than the way you've decided to go about arranging your quiet time. It's a structure, an outline, a model you are following.

That's all it is.

I prepared an outline when I began to write this book. It was my way of organizing my thoughts and arranging them in a way that makes sense. But guess what? I had to change that outline more than once before the book was finished.

Why?

Because I could not see into the future when I created the plan. It was my best guess for what would be helpful for me in writing this book. But it was only a guess. There were aspects of what I predicted might occur in my writing process that I was wrong about. Way wrong. So I had to make adjustments.

Your plan (even the ones you discover in this book) can become a straight-jacket if you let yourself believe that you cannot deviate from the plan.

So do you need a plan? I'd say "YES!". But do you have to always, without fail, stick to the plan? I'd say "NO!"

Allow yourself to be flexible with your plan day to day.

An example:

I had a great conversation about this with my 17 year-old daughter not too long ago. She was struggling in her time with the LORD each day because she felt she didn't have time to do everything she felt she should do. When I first heard her say that, I was shocked. This is a young lady who journals during her quiet time, so she spends well over an hour each day in her devotions and sometimes more (yes, she is home schooled).

When we got into the conversation I discovered that one of the issues that was causing her the most frustration was her prayer list. She had, with the best of intentions, created a list of people and things that she wanted to be regularly praying about. That's a very good thing to do (it's a plan). But she was feeling that if she didn't get to pray about every single issue on that list, every single day, she was somehow not living up to her end of some imaginary bargain she'd made with God.

I explained to her that the list is a plan. It's a goal, something you shoot for. But if you can't achieve it every day… well, then you can't achieve it. That's part of being human. We do the best we can, leaning on the LORD for direction and empowerment, and leave the resulting accomplishments and their results up to Him.

I saw the light go on when she was able to release the sense of obligation to get through the entire list and entrust it to the LORD. It was a beautiful thing.

So what about you? Do you have any belief that you have to stick to the plan no matter what? If you do, you'll wind up putting yourself in a straight-jacket.

## STRAIGHT-JACKET #2 – FORGETTING IT'S ABOUT RELATIONSHIP

This point is also part of what my daughter and I discussed. Daily time spent with the LORD is time spent with a PERSON. It's not an activity, an item on your "to do list," or a responsibility (at least not at the heart of it). Your daily quiet time is more like an appointment you make with your best friend. It's something you usually enjoy and that you look forward to.

Since your daily quiet time *is* about your relationship with the LORD, that means that your time with Him is by nature fluid, because relationship *are* fluid.

Think of the last conversation you had. You may have had specific things you wanted to talk about, but you didn't know exactly how the conversation was going to go, did you? You walked into it with some expectations and hopes, but likely walked away having experienced something at least slightly different in the end.

That is the nature of a relationship. It's flexible, dynamic, fluid. Your time with the LORD will be the same.

Each day, you meet with God for your special appointment, your plan represents *your* idea of how you'd like the conversation to go. But because both you and the LORD are persons, the way it actually goes will be at least a little bit different than that expectation. That's because you are both participants in the conversation, but also because there are situations going on in your life that are different from the month before (or even the day before). There may also be things He wants you to learn that day that He wasn't ready to reveal to you before. That's how relationships work. That is how personal growth works.

That is how your daily time with God has to work.

So how does this idea strike you? Have you forgotten that your daily quiet time is an appointment with a Person?

## STRAIGHT-JACKET #3: FORGETTING THAT GOD IS MERCIFUL

Too many of us act like (or only think that) missing our quiet time with God is going to take our name out of the Lamb's book of life.

You might think I'm exaggerating a bit too much there, and maybe I am, but let your mind ponder the idea for a moment.

Is it a "bad" thing to miss your quiet time? Well, is it?

Yes… mainly because we NEED that time with God every day. He is our source, our resource, and our life. We can't go without Him nearly as well as we think we can. Jesus said,

**John 15:5** – …apart from me you can do nothing.

He meant it, and I've learned it the hard way. What about you?

But missing our quiet time for some legitimate reason is not a bad thing in the sense that it is sinful. Life happens. We are fallen people. Things don't always go according to plan and we are not always reliable at implementing our plan. We will miss our quiet time from time to time.

*The point I'm getting to is this:* God understands all of that and the thousand other things that sometimes keep us from our daily appointments with Him. And more importantly, He is merciful toward us when we do miss.

Think of the last appointment with another human being that you missed. Was the person merciful about it? Nine times out of ten, people are merciful when we miss an appointment. Don't you think God is *at least* that merciful too? I have news for you; He's more merciful.

So, don't let yourself get straight-jacketed into thinking that an appointment with God that is missed is a mark against you in His book. If you let yourself believe that (see how mindset figures in again?) you'll actually become one of two things, or perhaps both:

- *A legalist who has no joy in the appointment. You do it because you have to do it.*

- *A slacker who avoids the appointment because you don't want to feel guilty when you finally stick to it because of all the other times you have missed it.*

God is merciful. A missed daily time with Him is not going to ruin your relationship with Him. He wants you coming to Him joyfully, and often. But when you miss, He's going to treat you like the perfect Father because that's what He is.

# MINDSET #4: SIMPLE MIND HACKS

In chapters ahead, I want to give you some practical, workable, effective methods that you can use in your daily Bible reading and quiet time with the Lord

BUT BEFORE WE GET THERE...let's consider some basic facts about good Bible study.

### UNDERSTAND THE VASTNESS OF YOUR GOAL

When you think of developing the habit of daily time with God,

what is your goal? Are you wanting to learn about God? Is it a time for you to come to understand the scriptures better? Are you hoping to strengthen your relationship with God?

In the end, your goal needs to be according to God's words spoken through Jeremiah, the prophet.

> **Jeremiah 9:23-24** Thus says the LORD: "Let not the wise man boast in his wisdom, let not the mighty man boast in his might, let not the rich man boast in his riches, but let him who boasts boast in this, that he understands and knows me, that I am the LORD who practices steadfast

love, justice, and righteousness in the earth. For in these things I delight, declares the LORD."

To know the LORD God is the most ambitious goal a human being can have. It's a vast goal, one that would literally blow your puny human mind if you ever accomplished it fully. Nevertheless, it's one we are to aspire to day after day after day… and your time with Him is a daily step toward that goal.

*Here's the problem…*

For many people, one of their main concerns about daily quiet time is how long it's going to take. After all, we're busy people. We have to be to work on time, to get the kids to soccer on time, to cook and clean the house, to get the car to the repair shop, and on and on and on.

Because of this we've adopted a "quick and easy" mindset about most things in life. We want the good things in life to come quickly and easily.

But relationship with God cannot be squeezed into such a tiny methodology. It's going to take time. It's going to take effort. It's going to take more than 5 minutes a day.

The main way that God has given us to know Him is through the scriptures. They teach us who He is, what He's like, what He's up to in the world (and history), and how we are to live in light of those things.

Think about it: God has been gracious enough to give you an entire book, composed of 66 individual documents. It's the largest book most of us will ever read (my Bible has 2,752 pages), and it reveals God and His ways to us.

In order for the great gift of God's scripture to be beneficial to us, they must be:

- *read*
- *understood*
- *and applied.*

You can't do all that in 5 minutes each day. The kind of benefit you need to derive from the scriptures, and that God intends, can only come as you invest the time to truly comprehend the Bible.

So, you need to get yourself into a mental place where you can say,

> *"I'm going to need to devote some time to this if I'm going to truly benefit."*

Once you are able to get your mind around that idea, you'll have overcome a huge hurdle and have put yourself in a place where you can stick with it day to day.

## START WITH PRAYER

To get started, I'd suggest that you always, always, **ALWAYS** begin your daily study time with prayer.

I don't mean that you need to take out your prayer list and pray for everyone from your spouse to your co-worker's Aunt Ethel. I'm talking about an introductory prayer, to set your mind in the right place (*Remember how important the mind is?*)

My insistence that you start here is based on two scriptural principles that go together. You can think of it as connecting the dots...

- *God Himself is eager to have a genuine relationship with you. He's proved it through the gift of His Son, Jesus. (John 3:16, Romans 5:8)*
- *God has promised that if you ask for anything He wants, He will give it. (1 John 5:14-15)*

So...

If God wants a relationship with you even more than you do (the first point), and if He has promised to give you the things He wants when you ask Him for them (the second point), then it makes perfect, divine, *powerful* sense that the most important thing you can do to establish a consistent and meaningful time with the LORD is to **ask Him** for it each day as you begin seeking Him.

**Plead - Beg - Ask - Seek - Knock - Pursue - Beseech (there's a King James word for you)**

And don't do it in a "wishful" sort of way (I sure wish this would happen...).

No, do it with CONFIDENCE! Jesus has made the way for you to go boldly before God's throne to ask Him for the help you need...

**<u>Ephesians 3:12</u> – In whom we have boldness and access with confidence through our faith in him.**

So start out by asking God to help you every day.

### SLOW DOWN

I mentioned the time issue a bit earlier. It's something you truly need to take into serious consideration. Your daily time with the LORD is not a race, a project, or a task where you get points for finishing early.

It's the exact opposite. You get more out of God's truth the longer you marinate in it. Human beings *can* marinate… it's called meditation. You need to take time to make that happen.

When you study the Bible you need to be taking time to understand:

- *the intricacies of the situations it describes.*
- *the logic in the arguments it makes.*
- *the deep spiritual truths that underlie the verbiage and sentences.*
- *the application it has to your life and relationships.*

That means it may take you a few days to digest only one passage or story. It may require that you write the key verses on a card and read and ponder them throughout the day (highly recommended!).

All of that is perfectly O.K. *Really.*

You need to get out of the "get er done" mindset. It's not important how fast you finish your scriptural meal, it's important how much nourishment you get from it!

That means you may have to do something practical (*gasp!*).

Make sure you schedule enough time to actually get something out of the meal. Five minutes won't do it. Ten minutes probably won't either.

God is worth it. Make enough time.

## REMEMBER THE BIBLE IS UNLIKE ANY OTHER BOOK

You can't simply read the Bible and "get it" immediately.

You need the LORD to reveal His will and ways to you as you consider the scriptures. His thoughts are much higher than yours, as are His ways (Isaiah 55:8-9).

> **For my thoughts are not your thoughts, neither are your ways my ways, declares the LORD. For as the heavens are higher than the earth, so are my ways higher than your ways and my thoughts than your thoughts.**

There's no hope of grasping the eternal and unfathomable riches that are recorded in scriptures unless you lean on Him in childlike dependence.

That ties in nicely with the prayer I mentioned previously. Only now I'm suggesting that you make it an ongoing practice as you read the scriptures.

- *When you hit something you don't get... ask God to explain it.*
- *When you are confused or unsettled by something... ask Him to give you insight and comfort.*

Interact with God as you read the scriptures. You need His help because the book He's given you is unlike any book you've ever read. You'll find Him more than willing to help you understand.

## REMEMBER THAT YOU'RE DEVELOPING A RELATIONSHIP

Any relationship takes time and effort, and none of them happen naturally or easily. The same is true of your relationship with the LORD.

It IS a relationship… you know that, don't you?

Your daily time with the LORD is not…

- *a religious act*
- *a ritual*
- *an obligation*
- *a box to be checked each day...*

It's a way that you engage in relationship with God, and it needs care and intentional attention.

It's a time to:

- *share*
- *listen*
- *interact*
- *and engage*

because it's part of developing a relationship... but with the living God of the universe!

## MAKE IT AN APPOINTMENT

There have been a handful of times in the course of my marriage that our family has had more month than money. Does that sound familiar?

During two different seasons when we were tight financially, I took a job delivering papers early in the morning. I can remember I had to rise at 3:30 in the morning, drive 30 miles to pick up the papers, and then deliver them house to house.

Because I'm pretty conscientious about work related things, I would pop out of bed when the alarm went off. It was a responsibility, and I tend to take work responsibilities pretty seriously. I was never late picking up the papers. I made it a priority. I set my mind before going to bed and when the alarm went off, I had already decided I would get out of bed.

One morning as I was out delivering papers, a new thought came to me about the struggle I'd been having in staying consistent in my daily quiet time. It went something like this...

Why is it that I am so quick to get out of bed for a job, but can't do the same thing to meet the King of the universe?

It was a powerful question, prompted by the Holy Spirit that helped me understand the priority that my daily time with the LORD needed to be. It was a question that radically changed my thinking (*remember the power of right thinking?*).

I intentionally began to think of my daily time with the LORD like I did work. It was something that I could not allow myself to miss.

***What about you?*** Would a mind-shift of that kind be helpful?

You can train yourself to think of each day's time with the LORD as an appointment, one that's important to you. Like a business related meeting or meeting with a friend for coffee. Whatever meetings or rendezvous are important to you, realize that your daily time with God is far, FAR more important and

DECIDE that you are going to treat it with the importance it deserves.

You just might be amazed at the impact it has...

# COMMON MINDSET MISTAKES

Because our mindset about our daily time with God is so critical, it makes sense that mistakes in how we think about it can cause some unwanted problems. The aim of this short chapter is to put some possible mindset mistakes on your radar, so you'll be aware of them and hopefully be able to avoid them.

### MISTAKE #1: I CAN BE A SLACKER BECAUSE GOD IS MERCIFUL

It's one thing to rightly understand that God is merciful when you miss your time with Him now and then. But it's quite another to miss it repeatedly because of neglect or carelessness or apathy and expect that His mercy makes it all better.

That's a cop-out for your own irresponsibility and laziness, and that *is* sin. Worse, it could be a sign that you don't truly care about your relationship with Him in the first place. Yes, I'm saying that an attitude like that *could* mean you are not a Christ-follower at all.

My logic on that goes something like this…

1. IF the Holy Spirit has come to live inside me,

2. THEN my life will begin to produce fruit that indicates that change has really taken place.

The Holy Spirit is not impotent. He is not lazy. He is not ineffective. He produces fruit in the lives of those He redeems. Scripture makes it very clear…

> **Matthew 7:17-18** – **So, every healthy tree bears good fruit, but the diseased tree bears bad fruit. A healthy tree cannot bear bad fruit, nor can a diseased tree bear good fruit.**
>
> **John 15: 6** – **You did not choose me, but I chose you and appointed you that you should go and bear fruit and that your fruit should abide, so that whatever you ask the Father in my name, he may give it to you.**
>
> **Romans 7:4** – **Likewise, my brothers, you also have died to the law through the body of Christ, so that you may belong to another, to him who has been raised from the dead, in order that we may bear fruit for God.**
>
> **Galatians 5:22-23** – **But the fruit of the Spirit is love, joy, peace, patience, kindness, goodness, faithfulness, gentleness, self-control; against such things there is no law.**
>
> **Colossians 1: 9-10** – **And so, from the day we heard, we have not ceased to pray for you, asking that you may be filled with the knowledge of his will in all spiritual wisdom and understanding, so as to walk in a manner worthy of**

**the Lord, fully pleasing to him, bearing fruit in every good work and increasing in the knowledge of God.**

Do you get the point? If you are a believer in Christ, you should expect your heart to be growing in its desire for time alone with God. You should expect that your desires for His word and for prayer will be increasing. You should expect that your ability will begin to grow to match your desires because the Holy Spirit is providing the power to make that happen.

So don't abuse the idea of mercy. You were made for more than that.

## MISTAKE #2: DEPENDENCE ON YOUR EMOTIONS

This one may sound strange to you, but believe me, it's very real. There are at least 4 ways dependence on your emotions could be seen in your life, but probably even a lot more than that.

### The "I'm just not feeling it" version

I have news for you. You won't wake up each morning enthused and excited about spending time with the LORD. Sometimes the bed will be more inviting. Other times you'll be eager to get started with work, jobs around the house… whatever. If you have your time with Jesus scheduled when you get home, you won't always feel you have the energy for it.

*The point is that days will come when you're just not feeling it. Does that mean you shouldn't do it?*

You need personal time with the LORD every day, and giving in to that feeling will be disastrous. Your day will be worse if you miss it, and your ability to honor the LORD with your life will be compromised – guaranteed.

Your desire or lack of desire at any given moment in time has absolutely nothing to do with whether or not you should meet with the LORD. You need that time, so depend on Him to help you, and do it.

### The "I'm not getting much out of it" version

The time you spend with the LORD each day may sometimes "feel" good while other times it may "feel" pretty dry. If it's the later, does that mean you didn't really spend quality time with God? Does it mean that something is wrong? Does it mean that you aren't "doing it right?"

Your emotions are likely to tell you a very loud "Yes" to every one of those questions.

While there may be some truth there to consider, it's not necessarily true all the time. You need to know that your feelings won't always line up with what is really happening between you and God… and that's O.K. Your feelings are not the barometer of truth, God is.

Your diligence and consistency to have consistent appointments with God will go a long way to overcome those negative feelings. In fact, over time, feelings tend to follow what you believe. So, if you are spending time with the Lord over His word, you can take the promises of His word to heart and believe them. Promises like these…

**Psalm 119:11** – I have stored up your word in my heart, that I might not sin against you.

**James 4:8** – Draw near to God, and he will draw near to you.

**Hebrews 10:22-23** – Let us draw near with a true heart in full assurance of faith, with our hearts sprinkled clean from an evil conscience and our bodies washed with pure water. Let us hold fast the confession of our hope without wavering, for he who promised is faithful.

You need to believe that when you draw near to God, He is drawing near to you, no matter what you feel about it. God has promised that your efforts to know Him better will not be in vain. You have confidence to draw near to God because Jesus has made the way for you to be reconciled to God. So, *"hold fast the confession of your hope without wavering, for he who promised is faithful."*

### The "I felt it so it must be true" version

I'm with you on the difficulty of this one. Emotions can be very convincing. But I've had many an emotional experience that I believed was from the LORD, only to find out later that the thing I was "feeling" I should do was not consistent with teaching already outlined in scripture.

When you do have an emotional experience with the LORD, make sure that you take your experience to the scriptures for evaluation. Your enemy the devil will be happy to give you all kinds of emotional experiences if they will detract you from living and acting according to God's truth.

I'm not saying emotional experiences are bad or wrong – far from it. I'm just cautioning you to keep the truth of God, as revealed in His word, alongside any experiences you may have. Let the word of God interpret, guide, and regulate what you conclude and believe about those kinds of feelings.

### *The "God doesn't want to talk to me" version*

When you have sinned, your feelings will try to convince you that you are "too guilty" or "too sinful" to go to God. Are you guilty? *As sin.*

But does that mean God doesn't want you to come to Him? Remember David's example in Psalm 51:17.

> **The sacrifices of God are a broken spirit; a broken and contrite heart, O God, you will not despise.**

It has been said that Martin Luther, the reformer once taught,

*Guilt only has one purpose, to drive you to the cross. Once you are there, its usefulness is gone.*

I couldn't verify that Luther ever said that, but what that statement says is still just as true. If you feel guilty because you have sinned, that means you're being nudged by the Holy Spirit to go to Jesus to get that sin taken care of. In that case, guilt is your friend.

Go to God in spite of what you feel, in brokenness and repentance. That is exactly the kind of heart He is looking for. He will receive you, forgive you, and restore you.

### *The "I'm doing this so God will be happy with me" version*

Legalism is believing that you can do something to gain God's favor, when the truth is that you can't. Do you really, really, REALLY know that to be true?

Here is the facts. If you have placed your faith in Jesus Christ, then you have God's favor by virtue of Jesus' death on the cross in your place. *Nothing more. Nothing less.*

When you think that your performance can somehow impact God's acceptance of you, you will begin to see a roadblock to your daily time with God, because you are believing something that is not true.

*For example:* You might be prone to spending a certain amount of time in Bible study, or a certain minimum amount of time in prayer before you "feel right" about making requests of the LORD.

Let's analyze that. Are you trying to butter God up with some good actions before you ask Him for what is really on your heart? That's legalism, alive and well in your devotional life.

God doesn't want your religious actions, He wants your heart.

> **Matthew 15:8 – This people honors me with their lips, but their heart is far from me.**

It matters more to God that you are honest when you come to Him than whether or not you do all the things *you think* He expects.

*The "I don't want to do it" version*

This one is laziness, pure and simple. What I'm going to cover is similar to the point about abusing God's mercy, but with a different twist.

We don't like to face up to it, but it's the sad truth about all of us from time to time. Sometimes we simply don't want to put in the effort it takes to get what we need from our time with the Lord. We want microwave, fast-food spirituality. Add water and stir.

But like many things in life, such as physical health, a good marriage, competence in your job, and a thousand other things, it takes diligent effort to achieve what is needed in your spiritual life.

What should you do if laziness is at the root of your problem? The answer to laziness is self-control. You have to be able to control your self.

But stop a second and remind yourself, as I mentioned earlier, true self-control comes from the Spirit of God. Galatians 5:22-23…

> **But the fruit of the Spirit is love, joy, peace, patience, kindness, goodness, faithfulness, gentleness, self-control; against such things there is no law.**

If you will turn to the Holy Spirit in an attitude of dependence and ask Him to give you self-control, He will give it. But as a friend of mine says,

*"You can sit naked on the bed all day long and God won't dress you."*

Once you've asked the Holy Spirit for self-control, your faith has to go to work! If you really believe that He will answer your prayer then begin doing what the Spirit would have you do as a self-controlled person.

You'll find that in the doing, He will provide the self-control you need. Remember what James 2:26 says,

> **...as the body apart from the spirit is dead, so also faith apart from works is dead.**

### *The "I feel so distracted" version*

For years I beat myself up over this one. I'd be as little as 5 or 10 minutes into my daily time with the LORD and something completely unrelated would come to mind. It might be something I had to do at work that day, or a conversation I had with my wife the night before, or a website I remembered I wanted to check out, or the hole in my sock (no joke)... and the list goes on!

I'd scold myself for being such a flake, failure, and baby Christian. Somehow I expected that I should be able to control my thoughts to the point that they would not wander.

You know what I came to realize? Having a distracted mind was not the problem.

Let me say that again: ***Having a distracted mind was not the problem.***

The problem was that I wasn't doing anything to manage the distractions that were sure to come. Here's how I took care of the problem once and for all… it's very, very simple. Are you ready?

***A note pad and a pencil.***

Seriously.

When the inevitable "to do" task invades your quiet time with the LORD, jot it down on your trusty pad with your trusty pencil, and go back to your conversation with God.

It really works. Writing it down helps you off-load that concern so that you can be free of its urgency. Just make sure you develop some kind of system so that you can be sure that you'll get back to that task and make sure it happens.

I still have a wandering mind, but it doesn't wander completely away now, because I've learned to off-load those stray thoughts in such a way that I'm confident that nothing important will go undone.

Give it a try, I'm pretty sure it will be of help to you too!

## MISTAKES CAN BE FIXED

If you find yourself putting a check mark next to one or more of these as problems you've experienced, you are in very good company. At one time or another I have struggled with all of them.

The good news is that now that you are aware of them you can enlist the help of the Holy Spirit to begin overcoming them. He'll be faithful to help you notice them, remind yourself of the truth, and step out with new behavior.

# *SECTION TWO: METHODS*

# THE S.O.A.P. METHOD

There are many ways to study the Bible.

At times you'll need to find something that "fits" your personality or bent. Other times you'll need a way to approach the scriptures differently to give you a fresh, re-energized perspective about your Bible study time.

This chapter begins the tools, the methods you can use to dig into the scriptures.

## THE S.O.A.P. BIBLE STUDY METHOD

This method is a "daily devotional" type study method that takes anywhere from 15 to 30 minutes per day, depending on the scripture passage you are using. As far as I know, this method was first devised by Pastor Wayne Cordiero of New Hope Fellowship on the island of Oahu, Hawaii.

### BENEFITS

- *You can have a meaningful time in the scriptures in a relatively short time.*
- *This method teaches you the basics of how to approach the scriptures wisely.*

- *It helps you develop the habit of daily scripture study without being overwhelming.*

## TOOLS YOU'LL NEED

- *A trustworthy Bible translation (ESV, NIV, NASB, NKJV, KJV, RSV)*
- *A notebook or journal*
- *A scripture reading plan that covers no more than 1 chapter of the scriptures daily.*

For your scripture reading plan, you can use a ready-made plan, or make up your own. You could even begin at the beginning of any Bible book and work through a chapter or less each day, depending on what fits your need.

## HOW TO DO IT

Each day's time in the scriptures will include 4 sections of focus, listed below...

**S – Scripture** – Read the scripture you have chosen for the day. Make sure you take the time to understand what is being said, who is saying it, and why they are saying it. In your notebook, hand write the part of the scripture that stands out to you. Taking the time to write it out will help you get it into your mind and heart.

**O – Observation** – Ask the Lord to teach you through the passage. What do you think He is saying to you through what you've read? Paraphrase and write down what you think He is telling you.

**A – Application** – Write out how the passage applies to your life. Again, the writing is important. Are there attitudes or actions you need to change in light of what you've read? Are there conflicts you need to resolve, promises you need to accept, or encouragement you need to receive?

**P – Prayer** – Ask the Lord to apply the truths of the passage to your heart. Ask Him for the strength you need to apply what you have learned with honesty.

The S.O.A.P method is a great starter plan, something to get you going in a way that is not too cumbersome or difficult. The only additional suggestion I'd make is that you write down the most meaningful part of the scripture for each day and take it with you for review throughout the day (note card, index card, etc.)

# METHOD #2

# THE SCRIPTURE/PRAYER METHOD

For most of my Christian life, my time in the scriptures has been good but my prayer time has been weak. In trying to figure out a routine for both that really worked for me, I stumbled upon this method of Bible study, *and it has worked tremendously!*

I've come to call it the *"Scripture and Prayer"* method because it centers around meditation on the scriptures and prayer as a response to what you have read and considered. It's one of my favorite ways to spend time with the LORD in the scriptures!

Before I give you a full-blown description of how the scripture and prayer plan works, there are two scriptural truths that have helped it to be of particular value to me. They may sound familiar, because I showed you a similar idea in the "prayer" section of chapter four.

Here it is:

- *God answers our prayers when we ask things He wants to give us (1 John 5:14).*
- *Our hearts are sick without Christ. We can't even have the right desires if God does not give them to us (Jeremiah 17:9, Romans 3:10-18)*

These two, very different scriptural truths combine to help me with this study method in two ways...

- *As I realize that I am unable to do what scripture is instructing me to do (Jeremiah 17:9, Romans 3:10-18), I find myself more dependent on God, and more eager to see Him work in my life to overcome my natural wretchedness.*
- *So, I ask Him to do in me what the passages instruct me to do... the very things I cannot do on my own. And believing that what He instructs me to be is what He desires me to be, I have great confidence that He will do what I'm asking Him to do, because I'm praying according to His will (1 John 5:14)*

Do you see how that works?

Those two truths have encouraged me in my daily walk with the LORD countless times. Because of them, I'm typically eager, hopeful, and excited to meet with Him. I can't wait to see what wonderful things He desires for me, that I will be able to understand and ask Him for as I meet with Him.

And I find myself more eagerly looking for His work being fulfilled in my life, because I know He will answer my prayers for these types of things!

## BENEFITS OF THE SCRIPTURE AND PRAYER METHOD

- *You will develop a greater appreciation for what the scriptures are saying.*
- *You will learn to pray biblical prayers, prayers that ask God for the things He delights to give to His children.*
- *You will be able to incorporate your personal Bible study and personal prayer together, with some*

limitations… in other words, you will be able to study the scriptures and pray during the same daily time. But your "prayer list" will have to be addressed in some other way.
- You can use any passage of the Bible, though the New Testament Epistles and the Psalms and Proverbs lend themselves to this method particularly well.

## TOOLS YOU'LL NEED

- A trustworthy Bible translation (ESV, NIV, NASB, NKJV, KJV, RSV)
- A notebook or journal, or a Bible with wider margins (I first began this method by writing things in my Bible margins, but have now decided to use a journal to record more extended thoughts and prayers.)

## HOW TO DO IT

- Read the passage you've selected, verse at a time, seeking to understand what the author is saying about God and His relationship with people/the world. Take it in bite-sized pieces.
- Jot down what the passage says about God's attitude toward people, His actions toward them, and what He requires or instructs in the passage.
- Pray the verse back to God, personalizing as you go (a brief example is below).
- Write out your prayer if that is helpful to you.

## EXAMPLE

**Psalm 1:1-2** – Blessed is the man who walks not in the counsel of the wicked, nor stands in the way of sinners, nor sits in the seat of scoffers; but his delight is in the law of the Lord, and on His law he meditates day and night.

> *Notes:* *I see that God Himself says that those who have association with people whose lives are characterized by wickedness or sin will not be blessed by Him. He blesses those who do not have those kinds of regular associations. God blesses those who delight in His law, those who meditate on His law consistently.*
>
> *Prayer:* *Father, make me to delight in Your word/Your law. Create in me the kind of heart that truly delights in the truths You have to say to me. Make my soul love it. Make my mind and heart crave it. Teach me how to seek Your will through Your word. Teach me how to apply it honestly. Give me the self-control and discipline to regularly, habitually meditate on Your word.*

Once you've completed this simple pattern, move on to the next section of your passage. One of the great things about this method is that it's very flexible. You can stop mid-way through a chapter if time does not allow you to continue, or you can do more if you are able.

# THE TOPICAL BIBLE STUDY METHOD

Topical bible study methods have been around for as long s the scriptures have been compiled into one book. It's an in-depth way of discovering what the scriptures say about any subject…

- *faith*
- *love*
- *hope*
- *joy*
- *perseverance*
- *anger*
- *holiness*
- *and on and on the list goes...*

The Bible contains wisdom about these subjects and thousands more.

If you are looking for an in-depth way of studying a specific subject, the topical bible study method is for you.

<u>BENEFITS OF TOPICAL BIBLE STUDY</u>

- *You'll gain a very comprehensive knowledge of a specific biblical topic.*
- *You'll become familiar with a large portion of scripture, in bite-sized pieces.*

## TOOLS YOU'LL NEED

- *An Exhaustive Concordance for your Bible version or*
- *Decent Bible Software (E-sword is a good one, and it's free - http://www.e-sword.net)*
- *A notebook or journal*

## HOW TO DO THE TOPICAL BIBLE STUDY METHOD

- *Choose your topic.*
- *Look up the topic in your concordance or with Bible software (a concordance in the back of a study Bible will only give you the most important or popular verses where the subject is addressed. To find every instance of a subject, you'll need to use an Exhaustive Concordance or Bible software).*
- *Using your Bible, look up the first verse you find about the subject. Read it. Seek to understand the situation and verses surrounding it. Write down what you discover that verse says about your topic.*
- *Move on to the next verse in your list and do the same.*
- *Continue through the list.*
- *As you go, you might find it helpful to categorize the ways the topic is spoken of, so that you can keep them separated in your mind.*

You may have figured this out by now, but let me say it clearly just in case.

The topical method can't be finished in one sitting.

In fact, depending on what subject you choose and how much time you devote to it in a given day, it could take a very long time. I've done studies in the past that took me well over a year of daily work with my concordance and Bible.

But don't let that intimidate or discourage you. Keep reminding yourself of the task you are about (getting to know God) and plug away at it. The insights and wisdom you'll gain are well worth the effort.

# METHOD #4

# JOURNALING STUDY

Keeping a journal was a practice many people did in days gone by. A large number of biographies you read are only possible because the subject of the book kept a journal, telling of their life's events and their inner thoughts.

But journaling can be more than a simple diary. It can be a tool for tremendous spiritual growth.

Dawson Trotman, founder of the Navigators (http://www.navigators.org) used to say,

> "Thoughts disentangle themselves when they pass through the lips and the fingertips."

In my life, this has been powerfully true.

When I journal, I am able to unwind my thoughts, get them out for me to see and consider, and in the end, I think better as a result. I often find myself able to express myself better in prayer, by journaling my prayers. And I'm also able to understand the Bible better when I use a journal to record my thoughts and impressions as I read, meditate, and study.

<u>HOW TO JOURNAL FOR BIBLE STUDY</u>

This method of Bible study centers around writing down your observations, impressions, and feelings as you read the scriptures. It is similar to both the "S.O.A.P." method and the "Scripture/Prayer" method, but not as structured.

One drawback to learning how to journal is that journaling typically takes a significant amount of time.

You may find yourself frustrated that you haven't finished with your passage or even a portion of it by the time your daily time limit is over. But don't let that discourage you from giving it a try. Many people find their study time comes alive as they learn how to journal.

### BENEFITS OF LEARNING HOW TO JOURNAL

- *Helps you think through what you are studying with great effectiveness*
- *For those who like to write, this method can be a real joy*
- *You'll find this method may help you retain more of what you study*

### TOOLS YOU WILL NEED

- *A Trustworthy Bible translation (ESV, NIV, NASB, NKJV, KJV, RSV)*
- *A journal or notebook*

### HOW TO JOURNAL

- *Choose your passage and begin reading*
- *Read enough to understand the context and situation of the passage*

- *Hand-write the first bite-sized section of what you've read*
- *Begin writing out your thoughts about the passage*
- *Include thoughts, feelings, impressions, questions, life situations it may apply to, examples in your own life that come to mind, other passages that you know relate, etc.*
- *There is nothing off limits*
- *Write it like a prayer or conversation with the Lord if that is helpful*
- *Prayerfully reread what you've written*
- *Add to it if more thoughts come to mind*
- *Finish with prayer, asking the LORD to use what you've read to accomplish His work in you.*

# METHOD #5

# THE QUESTIONS METHOD

This method of Bible study is actually a part of all the other methods, but deserves to be addressed all on its own because of how useful it can be when you focus on it more intently.

The Bible study questions method is exactly what it sounds like. You ask a series of questions about the passage you are considering to help you better understand the context and meaning.

## BENEFITS

- *This method will open up new doors of understanding for you.*
- *It's so easy, anyone can do it.*
- *It will force you to look at the context carefully so you can get a more complete understanding of the passage.*

## WHAT YOU WILL NEED

- *A trustworthy Bible translation (ESV, NIV, NASB, NKJV, KJV, RSV).*
- *A journal or notebook (optional).*

## *HOW TO DO IT*

- *Read the passage you've chosen.*
- *Begin to ask questions about the passage:*
- *WHO is speaking?*
- *WHO are they speaking to?*
- *WHAT are they saying?*
- *WHY are they saying it?*
- *WHAT importance does it have?*
- *WHAT is the main point of what is being said?*
- *WHEN was this said (in history, in the story, etc.)?*
- *WHAT is being said about behaviors, attitudes, or heart motives?*
- *WHAT does it say to me, my situations, my life?*
- *WHAT is happening in me as I begin to understand this truth?*
- *DOES the passage reveal God's thinking or heart about a subject?*
- *DOES it show me something I should change in my life?*
- *WHAT does the passage reveal about God?*
- *AND ANY OTHER QUESTIONS THAT COME TO MIND...*
- *Write down the answers to the questions you ask (optional).*

Do you get the point? (Another question there... get it?)

These are only suggested questions; you could ask thousands of questions about every passage you read. Feel free to make up your own! You'll find that you understand the passage to a much greater degree as you ask and answer questions about it.

# METHOD #6

# THE 30 DAY PER BOOK METHOD

This method can change your life, and that's not an exaggeration! If you will dedicate yourself to practicing this method regularly, making the time everyday to carry it out, you'll see yourself growing in…

- *knowledge of God's word*
- *understanding of God's ways, and*
- *deep knowledge of His heart*

Sound too good to be true? Keep reading (and give it a try) and you'll see.

This is a method of Bible study that my daughter Melinda brought home from college. Unbelievably, in over twenty years as a Pastor I'd never heard of this idea before. It's a method so simple, yet so profound I am amazed.

One of Melinda's instructors at Bible college encouraged the students to follow this method. Melinda gave it a try and she loves it!

<u>HOW TO DO IT</u>

- *Choose a reliable Bible translation (KJV, ESV, NKJV, NIV, NASB)*
- *Choose a book of the Bible you want to use for your Bible reading for the next 30 days.*
- *HINT: This method works better with smaller books, like the epistles or groupings of the Psalms or Proverbs.*
- *Do your daily Bible reading by reading the ENTIRE book every day for 30 days.*
- *Jot down notes about things the LORD shows you.*

And that's it.

Pretty simple, huh?

But can you see how powerful it could be?

### BENFITS

- *Saturating yourself in a single book of the Bible for a prolonged period of time, you'll be soaking up the benefits and blessings of what God has to say in that particular book.*
- *You'll get God's truth in context, day after day so that you'll begin to understand the logic behind what the book is teaching.*
- *You'll become much more familiar with that particular book, so much so that it will readily come to mind throughout the day.*

Try this method. Your daily Bible reading will come alive in ways you never considered.

# METHOD #7

# A PRAYER SYSTEM THAT WORKS

SITUATION 1: You see a Christian brother while you are out and about and he shares an urgent prayer request with you. His need truly tugs at your heart so you tell him, "I'll be praying for you." But he's the hundredth person you've told that to in the past month, and you don't really have a way to keep up with all the requests.

SITUATION 2: You want to be a man or woman of prayer. You want to be regular, devoted, and effective in your prayer life. But it seems to overwhelming. There are so many things to pray about, and so much possibility of forgetting those important requests. It's discouraging.

SITUATION 3: You know you should be praying for your spouse and children more than you are, but life is just so busy. It seems that most of the time the best you can do is to throw up quick emergency prayers to God when a situation arises and go on with the frantic pace of life. You want to be more intentional in your prayers for those you love, but don't really know where to start.

*Do any of those scenarios sound familiar?*

To be honest with you, I've experienced every one of them at one time or another. It's a very strange struggle we Christians face. We want to be men and women of prayer, but prayer is hard to manage in a practical way. We want to be consistent, diligent, and devoted, but find that the task seems too overwhelming.

In this chapter I'm going to quickly outline a "prayer system" that I've discovered that can help with all of those problems. It's not foolproof and it will need tweaking from time to time, but overall, it will help you get your prayer life on the tracks and rolling.

## ORGANIZING

Like anything else, your prayer life is going to need some kind of organization. We'd all like to think that we can be those "spiritual giants" who pray naturally and consistently throughout the day but it's simply not the way it is. Overcoming the power of sin is a struggle even for us Christians and we need tools to help us build new habits.

So, organizing your prayers is the place to begin.

If you're like me, there are probably 30 or 40 significant prayer requests or situations that you'd like to be praying for on a regular or even daily basis. But to sincerely pray for 30 requests per day in one sitting will keep you away from most of the other God-given responsibilities in life. So, what do you do?

You put a system in place.

## MY CHANGE IN THINKING

For a long time I was convinced that if I didn't make it through my entire prayer list every day, I was a failure. But that wasn't true. I didn't need to feel pressured that every prayer needed had to be covered every day. I just needed to be consistent. What mattered was that in my heart I wanted to pray for those things regularly.

What I discovered is that if I put all my prayer items into an easy-to-follow system, I could do just that.

## THE SYSTEM I FOUND

Here's the simple explanation of how I've organized my prayer lists. I'll go into a bit more detail after I explain the overview.

- I've created two groupings of cards. The first is my "daily" prayer items and the second are my "rotating" prayer items.

- Each day, I take out both sets of cards.

- As you have already figured out, the "daily" group is what I try to pray for every day. These are usually family members(a card for each) or some pressing personal need or burden from the LORD. So, every card in that stack is prayed for every day (with some exceptions at times, which I'll speak to in a moment).

- The "rotating" group are items/requests that I pray for on a rotating basis. So, I'll take ONE of those cards and pray for the things I've listed on it. How many things are listed on it are up to me (no rules here). When I'm finished praying for those items, it goes to the back of the stack and I put the stack away.

So the way it winds up looking is that each day I'm praying through the entire "daily" stack, and one of the "rotating" cards. When I'm able to accomplish this I can honestly say that I'm praying for my family daily and other requests/needs on a regular basis.

Here is a picture of what my two sets of cards look like...

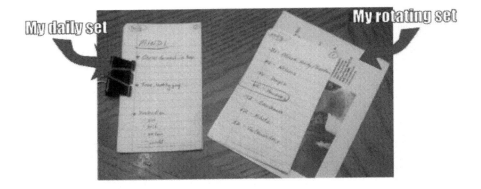

you'll notice that on my rotating set I have things broken up by day of the week, so that each week, I'm praying for a particular request on a particular day of the week. Notice also, I'm using paper clips or binder clips to keep the cards together. It doesn't have to be fancy, it just has to work!

## SOME EXCEPTIONS

I mentioned that there are exceptions to the "daily" aspects of my prayer routine. What I mean is this: life happens. There are days when I simply don't have the time to get to these prayers in such a systematic format. On days like that I ask the LORD to bring the requests to mind throughout the day and I pray for them when I'm able. Or, I might take the group of cards with me and put them in a shirt pocket or on the dash of my car. That way they are accessible to me as I go about my day and I don't have to rely on my memory to know what to pray for.

This prayer system has been a great encouragement to me. I'm no longer frustrated with the regularity of my prayer life. I'm no longer leaving out important prayer issues. It's working for me, generally speaking.

## SOME TWEAKS YOU'LL HAVE TO MAKE

I've just described how I go about using this system. You'll need to customize it to you and your own schedule. Here are some of the things you'll have to decide:

- *How many daily cards are you able to get to realistically? Don't overwhelm yourself with too many.*

- *How many items should you put on each day's "rotating" card? Again, don't destroy the helpfulness of the system by overloading yourself.*

- *How will you remember to add an item to your daily or rotating list? For me, I seldom add to my daily list since they are things like family members, etc. that don't change often. But my rotating list has things added to it often. I had to find a way to integrate that task into my daily task management system that I use for the rest of life. How will you do it?*

- *How will you decide when it's time to modify a request or remove it from your list altogether?*

As you can see, there are some variables you're going to have to figure out. But none of them are so difficult that it can't be done.

Again, this system has enabled me to pray consistently, be encouraged, and to honestly be able to say to folks that I'm praying for their requests and needs.

I hope it's helpful to you too.

# SECTION THREE: WRAP-UP

# My "normal" Daily Quiet Time System

Honestly, it's hard to say that my daily time with God has anything "normal" about it. That's because I work hard to keep it fresh, which means I might skip what is typical for the sake of doing something new or different. But overall, I do follow a certain pattern, which typically includes the use of two of the methods I've covered in this book.

Before I tell you what I do most of the time, let me say this...

This works for me. It may not work for you. You need to find your own "normal."

## MY NORMAL

I typically follow the scripture/prayer method combined with the journaling method. I also utilize the "note pad" idea to make sure that I keep track of the random things that hit my brain as I'm trying to interact with the LORD. My version of a "notepad" is my tablet, through which I can easily jot notes into my online task management system so they are not forgotten. (CAUTION: If you use an electronic device like I do, the added distraction of email / social media, etc. will be there. Prepare yourself for that.)

Here are some pictures of how it looks for me. First, I'll show you my overall setup:

I keep my prayer cards, journal, and some pens in a zipped pouch like this one so that everything I need is together. I'd recommend you find some way to keep the things you need together also.

And one last thing I try to do… since I try to keep my daily appointment with the LORD each morning, I put these things, along with my Bible, out on the table where I sit when I meet with Him. That way I'm not making noise in the room where my wife is typically still sleeping. But it's also helpful because everything I need is right there. It cuts down on excuses and eliminates obstacles simply by thinking ahead.

That's it. Pretty simple but very do-able.

How are you going to organize your appointments with the LORD?

# YOU CAN DO THIS

This book is short; intentionally so. I don't want to bog you down with too much information or too many ideas.

I want you to be able to grab onto some simple but workable tools and get yourself rolling toward a deeper and more beneficial relationship with God.

You need to know that I'm nothing special. I'm a punk kid who grew up in Texas who's struggled to know the LORD just like you have. I've had failures (colossal failures) and I've had victories. But no matter which came my way, God gave me the grace not to give up.

You can't give up either.

God's promises are true…

> **Proverbs 8:17** – I love those who love me, and those who seek me diligently find me.

> **Jeremiah 29:13** – You will seek me and find me, when you seek me with all your heart.

> **Amos 5:4** – For thus says the LORD to the house of Israel: "Seek me and live;

The LORD Himself will honor and energize your efforts to meet with Him regularly. You can count on it.

Do your part and watch for how He does His.

You will be amazed. ***Don't give up.***

GOD:POWER

# OTHER BOOKS BY CAREY GREEN:

**The Marriage Improvement Project** - a daily study for couples to experience together. The MIP leads husbands and wives into a deeper understanding of the purpose and structure of marriage and the responsibilities each of them has in the relationship. Filled with practical exercises and discussion questions for the couple to complete together, the MIP is a powerful way for a couple to learn God's truth about their relationship together. It's recommended that each partner have their own copy. - http://amzn.com/B00A6Z5K9A

**The Elder Training Handbook** -This guide for identifying and equipping men for the role of Elder is powerfully practical... from assessment to evaluation to installation. This workbook-style handbook is designed to help church leaders do just that, in a wise, careful, and thoroughly Biblical way. This handbook is not offered as a magic formula or fool-proof method for finding or equipping men for the role of Elder. No such thing exists. Scripture clearly teaches that men are only appointed to the role of Elder by the determination of the Holy Spirit (Acts 20:28). Instead, this handbook is designed to serve as a tool in that Spirit-led process. It is an aid in discerning the will of the Spirit, first through assessment of the man being considered, and secondly through training for those who appear to be called to serve as Elders. With over 260 study questions, a variety of self-assessment tools, scripture memorization, and "quizzes" to test the candidate's understanding and application of the concepts included, The Elder Training Handbook is a serious-minded tool for discovering, encouraging, and equipping men to shepherd, protect, and lead the New Testament church. - http://amzn.com/1475137559

**The Great Smizzmozzel Bash** - Your children will love this rollicking, rhyming, adventure - in the spirit of Dr. Seuss! The Great

Smizzmozzel Bash is a retelling of the origin of the Great Smizzmozzel Bash, held every year in the Jungles of Boon! Find out how the mysterious Smizzmozzel saves the day, the jungle, and the elephant King! Fun for the whole family! - http://amzn.com/B00AL4LIWE

**Dragon Slayer: Beginnings (a Christian novel)** -Dragons have been forgotten, relegated to the realm of legend and myth. But tales of horror circulate among the common people. Rumors of their attacks float on the night wind. They are a fearsome presence that haunts the memories of the old and the nightmares of the young. *They are forgotten, but they are not gone.*

The dragon masters wait, a dark force lurking in the shadows of every land. They will have their opportunity. *They will rise.*

A young boy is stripped violently from his family and thrust into the conflict between dragon masters and feudal lords. Through tragedy and loss Hon is swept into the conflict while battling the fear and pain that grips his own soul.

*Dragon Slayer: Beginnings* is a story of life and the growth of faith in the midst of loss. It's about the battle every person goes through to become more than their past has destined them to be.

*He is the first. He will be the best. He is the Dragon Slayer.*

*http://www.dragonslayerbook.com*

## REPRINTED BY CAREY GREEN:

**Horatio Alger's Pacific Series - 3 books in one!** - The entire "Pacific" series all in one book (never before provided). This copy contains the original text of all three book texts ("The Young Adventurer," "The Young Miner," and "The Young

Explorer" along with an additional original biography of Horatio Alger. Some words have been updated for modern readers. Horatio Alger's adventure books were loved by millions back in the 1800s... and their timeless lessons of courage, honesty, and hard work are of tremendous benefit to us today. This is a compilation of 3 of Alger's books, known as the "Pacific" series. They are filled with adventure, danger, challenges, and stories of boys rising from difficult situations to great success. The lessons learned here are invaluable skills to help children grow. - http://amzn.com/B00EMN094S

# CHRISTIAN HOME AND FAMILY

## *Equipping you to build a legacy of faith*

This book is a publication of Christian Home and Family at **http://www.ChristianHomeandFamily.com** . There you can find an ever-growing collection of free resources designed to equip your family toward a legacy of generational Christian faith. Please look over the site... you'll find other resources like this, our weekly "Conversation Starters for Couples" email resource - **http://www.ChristianHomeandFamily.com/list/** - and many, many other resources.

Made in the USA
Middletown, DE
08 January 2017